1 MONTH OF
FREE
READING

at
www.ForgottenBooks.com

By purchasing this book you are eligible for one month membership to ForgottenBooks.com, giving you unlimited access to our entire collection of over 700,000 titles via our web site and mobile apps.

To claim your free month visit:

www.forgottenbooks.com/free238418

ISBN 978-0-483-36892-7
PIBN 10238418

THE·HOVSE·OF·A HVNDRED·LIGHTS

BY·FREDERIC·RIDGELY·TORRENCE

SCIRE QVOD SCIENDVM

SMALL·MAYNARD & COMPANY
BOSTON

TO EDMUND CLARENCE STEDMAN
WITH REVERENCE AND LOVE

THE HOUSE OF A HUNDRED LIGHTS: A PSALM OF EXPERIENCE AFTER READING A COUPLET OF BIDPAI

1

On the pond's face, the pelting rain
   made bubbles, and they broke again,
And reappeared and disappeared
   and, ah! I knew them — they were men.

2

The wise men say that life's not worth
   a barley-corn when all is done.
Well, then — and not till then — I'll try
   the granary behind the sun.

3

"Doubt everything," the Thinker said
   when I was parch'd with Reason's drought.
Said he, "Trust me, I've probed these things;
   have utter faith in me, — and doubt!"

4

" Though the sky reel and Day dissolve,
    and though a myriad suns fade out,
One thing of Earth seems permanent
    and founded on Belief : 'tis — Doubt.

5

The world's great rule is, " Give and take";
    and, so that Custom may not smother,
I'll give Doubt freely with one hand
    and take Faith freely by the other.

6

Yes, He that wove the skein of Stars
    and poured out all the seas that are
Is Wheel and Spinner and the Flax,
    and Boat and Steersman and the Star.

7

What ! doubt the Master Workman's hand
    because my fleshly ills increase ?
No; for there still remains one chance
    that I am not His Masterpiece.

8

Out of all Epicurus' train
   I wonder which class is sincerest:
The drones, or workers, who believe
   this doctrine of " Believe-The-Nearest."

9

Though man or angel judge my life
   and read it like an open scroll,
And weigh my heart, I have a judge
   more just than any — my own soul.

10

The Great Inn Keeper's table is
   the whole green face of Earth, and so
I sit at meat with Him nor care
   whether the Guest be friend or foe.

11

The wise man said, " Beware of Love;
   behold, its end is Ash and Rue! "
" Ho, ho," cried Youth, " this heart of mine
   is braver than I ever knew."

12

Last night I heard a wanton girl
   call softly down unto her lover,
Or call at least unto the shade
   of Cypress where she knew he'd hover.

13

Said she, " Come forth, my Perfect One;
   the old bugs sleep and take their ease:
We shall have honey overmuch
   without the buzzing of the bees."

14

Ah, Foolish Ones, I heard your vows
   and whispers underneath the tree.
Her father is more wakeful than
   she ever dreamed, for I — was he.

15

I saw them kissing in the shade
   and knew the sum of all my lore:
God gave them Youth, God gave them Love,
   and even God can give no more.

16

At first, she loved nought else but flowers,
　　and then — she only loved the Rose,
And then — herself alone, and then —
　　she knew not what, but now — she knows.

17

Ah, Flattery, thou'rt like a comb
　　with double face and double tongue,
These women wear thee on their brows
　　like an asp coilèd where it stung.

18

The lies men tell I can see through —
　　they hold no more than does a sieve :
But women's lies hold like the sea,
　　and like it surge and swell and live.

19

Hot Youth, to know Contented Love,
　　must first bide Slander's rude caress,
And learn to quench his Fire-of-Rage
　　in Water-of-Babes-Gentleness.

20

The night passed and some youths caroused
    and some poor Fakir kept his fast:
Some lovers kissed, some graves were dug,
    all the same night, and the night—passed.

21

I know not from the fading Rose
    with parted lips what whisper went.
I only know the Nightingale
    Sang once again his old lament.

22

A nightingale once lost his voice
    from too much love, and he who flees
From Thirst to Wine-of-his-Desire
    must not forget the last — the lees.

23

Night is a woman vaguely veiled
    and made to woo, I see her now:
The newborn moon is suddenly
    her slender, golden, arched eyebrow.

24

I know a Thief who longs to steal
    from the moon's granary on high
Or snatch the bunch of Pleiades
    from out the cornfield of the sky.

25

Desire's gold gates are always barred
    and open at no call or knock.
Age knows the only key is Pain,
    but Youth still thinks to force the lock.

26

You invalids who cannot drink
    much wine or love, I say to you:
" Content yourselves with laughing at
    the antics of the fools who do."

27

Bad-Liver says each morning's sun
    is but to him a juggling bawd
That opens up for man's deceit
    only another chest of fraud.

28

Old Ash-in-Blood still deals advice
  to Rose-of-Youth, and as he deals it,
Rolls piously his eyes; but ah!
  he knows the pain whose body feels it.

29

"Now (to be brief)," the Preacher said,
  " each chose, himself, the path he's wending;
But has each thought upon the end?"
  And Youth said, "Is there then an ending?"

30

Five senses have been given us
  but while Youth pipes its roundelay
They are five open doors through which
  both Love and Life may slip away.

31

Youth dreamed that Chaos swallowed Space,
  Time's iron chain was snapped like rope,
Eternity passed, and was gone,
  yet after all these things came — Hope.

32

But now where is that faggot-heap
  of hope wherewith my youth began?
Fate was the flint and Time the steel
  that kindled every thought and plan.

33

In youth my head was hollow, like
  a gourd, not knowing good from ill;
Now, though 't is long since then, I'm like
  a reed, — wind-shaken — hollow still.

34

The reader in Life's mighty book,
  in quest of Happiness, the bubble,
Ne'er sees the Writing of Content
  without the heavy blot of Trouble.

35

The same small windows light all lives
  whether they be of rich or poor:
A sigh, a laugh, some wine, a sleep,
  a tear, and then — the open door.

36

Yes, we do sleep and dream and laugh,
  and yes, we wake and work and sigh;
I simply mumble now, " We do ";
  the watchword of my youth was, "Why?"

37

Age lays its ear unto the lips
  of Mortal-Man's-Experience
And only drinks the four faint words
  of Where and How and Why and Whence.

38

Tell Youth to play with Wine and Love
  and never bear away the scars!
I may as well tilt up the sky
  and yet try not to spill the stars.

39

Yet even for Youth's fevered blood
  there is a certain balm here in
This maiden's mouth: O sweet disease!
  and happy, happy medicine!

40

And maiden, should these bitter tears
   you shed be burdensome, know this:
There is a cure worth all the pain
   — to-night — beneath the moon — a kiss.

41

Girl, when he gives you kisses twain,
   use one, and let the other stay;
And hoard it, for moons die, red fades,
   and you may need a kiss — some day.

42

One says, " Truth's false and false is true."
   Well, since I've seen this maiden's eyes,
I'll be so false as to be true,
   and such a fool as to be wise.

43

These three have never yet been bought
   or sold within the market place, —
Good Luck or Love or Youth for gold
   of any of the populace.

44

Said one young foolish mouth with words
    as many as the desert sands,
" My grandfather took daily baths
    in rose water, just smell my hands!"

45

When priests give draughts of Duty's bowl
    and all streams that proceed from thence,
The old men do not drink with youths:
    they drink Advice, the young — Offense.

46

Brothers, to-day Time set a feast,
    for this day Summer was begun;
And by a priest called Equinox
    the Year was married to the Sun.

47

And now young poets will arise
    and burst Earth's fetters link by link,
And mount the Skies of Poesy,
    and daub Time's helpless wings with ink!

48

In youth I wrote a song so great,
  I thought that, like a flaring taper,
'T would shine abroad, — and so it did,
  to the four corners of the — paper.

49

And poet, should you think your songs
  must or even will be read,
Bethink thee, friend, what fine springs rise
  impotently from the sea's bed.

50

Fame sets the pace: the more you chase,
  the more she'll turn and taunt and flee,
Till you stand breathless at the goal
  and read its name, " Obscurity."

51

I did not hate that orator
  of many words for what he said :
I only thought it just some old
  quaint game his tongue played with his
    head.

52

I marveled at the speaker's tongue
  and marveled more as he unrolled it.
How strange a thing it was, and yet,
  how much more strange if he could hold it!

53

A little Judge once said to me:
  "Behold, my friend, *I* caused these laws!"
But I knew One who, strange to say,
  had been the Causer of this Cause.

54

And my conceited friend, be sure
  when you sleep, others will arouse;
For the Great Landlord can't endure
  to have no tenants in His house.

55

Many a word caused many a tear
  between the rise and set of sun;
Many a sound caused many a sigh
  but Silence rarely caused a one.

56

The Tabor is the noisiest
  of instruments, but take the pest
And crack his hide and peer within,
  you'll find his heart is hollowest.

57

Uhfus rehearsed before his goat,
  and practiced speech each day above it,
Until his fame spread far and wide,
  and yet — the goat — knew nothing of it.

58

The villagers laugh at their fool,
  and roar and cough and shake and nurse
Their aching sides, then laugh again;
  but he — laughs at the villagers.

59

This raindrop makes me dream brave dreams
  of how to overcome the sea:
The drop's far wiser head dreams too
  its dream, Impossibility.

60

When I'm in health and asked to choose
    between the This and That, alas!
I all too gladly yield my throne
    up there beside the Sea of Glass.

61

The Song of Love, the Song of Hate,
    the Songs of Praise and of Thanksgiving;
I've learned them all, but there remains
    one called the Melody of Living.

62

A strong, brave man is born each month,
    each year God gives a sage to men,
A poet each ten years, perhaps,
    but an unselfish person, — when?

63

Sometimes I think that all mankind
    exist but to be bought and sold:
The rich man's paramour is gold,
    the poor man's goddess, gold, gold, gold.

64

Whatever Juice this sky will pour
   this gaping parched old throat will drain;
What time the Harper harps I'll dance:
   'tis He, not I, who shall complain.

65

Meal may be scarce and cakes be burnt,
   yet I weep not nor even scold:
The sun is food enough for me,
   't is large, and has not yet grown cold.

66

And yet, when eventide comes on
   I know that I'll be glad to take
A little wine with snow, and yes
   (after the sun), a little cake.

67

Why! 'mongst all languages of earth
   there's none so sweet nor yet so fine
As that one spoken daily thrice
   by two and thirty teeth of mine.

68

Yet what have I to do with sweets
   like Love, or Wine, or Fame's dear curse?
For I can do without all things
   except — except the universe.

69

The sieve-like cup of Earthly Joy
   still foams for me with many a bead,
But I have found another wine
   called Charity-without-a-Creed.

70

And if I want to sleep, I'll sleep
   more than Religion's laws allow.
We'll have a long sleep in the grave
   erelong; and should we not learn how?

71

Whether my days are cooled with calm
   or filled with fever's ardent taint,
I have the same blue sky as God,
   I have the same God as the saint.

72

When strangers sit at meat with me,
   e'en though they be of rich condition,
And all their words be feasts, I'll take
   them with the little spice — Suspicion.

73

In all the undertakings I
   have entered in, my stratagem
Has been to widen carefully
   some gap for getting out of them.

74

I answer to the riddle of
   " How many men on earth should be?"
" For friends, a billion are too few;
   for enemies, — one surfeits me."

75

I make no truce with cunning foes,
   beneath their sweetest words lurk thorns,
But with all fools I am at peace:
   whoever saw an ass with horns?

76

Though all I was seems but a dream,
   and all I am, not worth a sigh,
If all that I possess is — friends,
   well, all I wish is — not to die.

77

I give God praise because of right,
   and fear, for terrors that He sends;
But more than all, I give Him love
   because He gave to me — my friends.

78

When I get wounds from enemies
   I try not to lament a bit:
The tree that bears not any fruit,
   who ever threw a stone at it?

79

When Fortune sits at meat with me
   and lights my fire and tolls my bell,
Be very sure I'll soon collect
   all scattered Means-of-doing-Well.

80

Ye wily ones think not to thwart
    what warrant Destiny hath signed ;
For just before he strikes, he makes
    the cunningest both deaf and.blind.

81

But work a year and sleep an hour,
    and sleep a night and sing a day,
And take a little wine and love,
    and when you feel religious — pray.

82

So far, alas, the desert bears
    the Caravan of the Wise and Just,
The wind brings to these foolish ones
    no sound of it, nor scent, nor dust.

83

For some are beasts and some are men
    in these new days as in the olden,
For neither now nor evermore
    will gold be clay or clay be golden.

84

Think not such sterile leaves of chaff
  have ever yet escaped the flail,
For on Fate's dreadful threshing floor
  Contrivance is of no avail.

85

Sea fathoms deep midst gold and gems
  Life sits and weeps on ocean's floor,
But though on land no treasure is,
  Life laughs and stands—I'll stay on shore.

86

I envied the brown diver when
  he brought the pearl to where I read,
But envy had not known my heart
  when the green waves closed o'er his head.

87

E'en though I be but thorns and dust
  the Gard'ner gives me as He goes
Such rains and suns, I give Him blooms,
  yes — perchance — even — a Rose.

88

Whether I be a blossom for
    the Gardener's nostrils I care not;
Mayhap I'll be the stick of wood
    that feeds the fire to boil His pot.

89

Now Patience is the hurtfullest
    of all the thorns my Garden wears,
And yet the sweetest of them all
    is the white bud that Patience bears.

90

This mess of cracked ice, stones and bread
    of sweetness savours not a bit,
And yet my friends, I'm satisfied,
    for lo! I — I — invented it!

91

When my desire has set itself
    upon a thing and strives to win it,
And Wisdom's method's will not gain,
    I use a little Folly in it.

92

Now all ye slothful ones, who fear
   Death's nearing goal, take heart of grace:
Who never went upon the road
   will never reach the halting place.

93

Let me once see my Spring of Hope
   clad in her clinging, light green dress,
Then I, for one, will aye endure
   my yellow Autumns of Distress.

94

Now who will undertake to tie
   this broken strand of yellow hair?
Ah! Is it tied, and strong? But friend,
   forget not this,—the knot is there.

95

Sometimes I think man's fate is like
   a weather vane with circling base
That points now north, now south, now turns,
   blown by the winds of Time and Space.

96

The Great Sword Bearer only knows
    just when He'll wound my heart, not I:
But since He is the one who gives
    the balm, what does it signify?

97

If my Control should lose its hold
    on Fortune's collar through some hurt,
What then?—Why then I'd simply cling
    to old grey Resignation's skirt.

98

Of all the languages of earth
    in which the human kind confer
The Master Speaker is the Tear:
    it is the Great Interpreter.

99

Man's life is like a tide that weaves
    the sea within its daily web.
It rises, surges, swells and grows,
    —a pause—then comes the evening ebb.

In this rough field of earthly life
   I have reaped cause for tears enough,
Yet after all, I think I've gleaned
   my modicum of Laughing-Stuff.

OF THIS FIRST EDITION OF THE
HOUSE OF A HUNDRED LIGHTS BY
FREDERIC RIDGELEY TORRENCE
WITH DECORATIONS AND COVER
DESIGN BY BERTRAM GROSVENOR
GOODHUE SEVEN HUNDRED AND
FIFTY COPIES HAVE BEEN PRINTED
FROM TYPE FOR SMALL MAYNARD
& COMPANY AT THE HEINTZEMANN
PRESS IN BOSTON U. S. A. IN THE
MONTH OF NOVEMBER MDCCCXCIX

The Heintzemann Press Boston